THE COMING OF THE KING

Fiona MacMath · Illustrated by Francesca Pelizzoli

OLIVER-NELSON PUBLISHERS
Nashville

GOD, who in certain times and in different ways spoke through the prophets, has spoken to us by his Son, says Hebrews 1: 1–3. The people of Israel had waited in hope for the Messiah who would save them from all their sins and sorrows, but only a few people still waited. Then one night, so surprisingly that few recognized him, He did come, a helpless baby in the straw.

Jesus was like the words of God made into a person that people could touch and see. He was someone who could explain what God was like and make good things happen in a troubled world.

Until Jesus came, people were "walking in darkness," trying to live as the Law of Moses taught them, but often disobeying it, often confused about what God really wanted. Jesus coming into the world was like God coming in and switching on the light. Not everyone likes the light — there are people who like the darkness to hide the evil things that they do. Often the darkness seems to have swallowed up the light completely, but it never has.

> In Him was life, and the life was the light of men....
> There was a man sent from God whose name was John.
> This man came for a witness to bear witness of the Light,
> that all through him might believe.
> And the Word became flesh
> and dwelt among us, and we beheld His glory,
> the glory as of the only begotten of the Father.

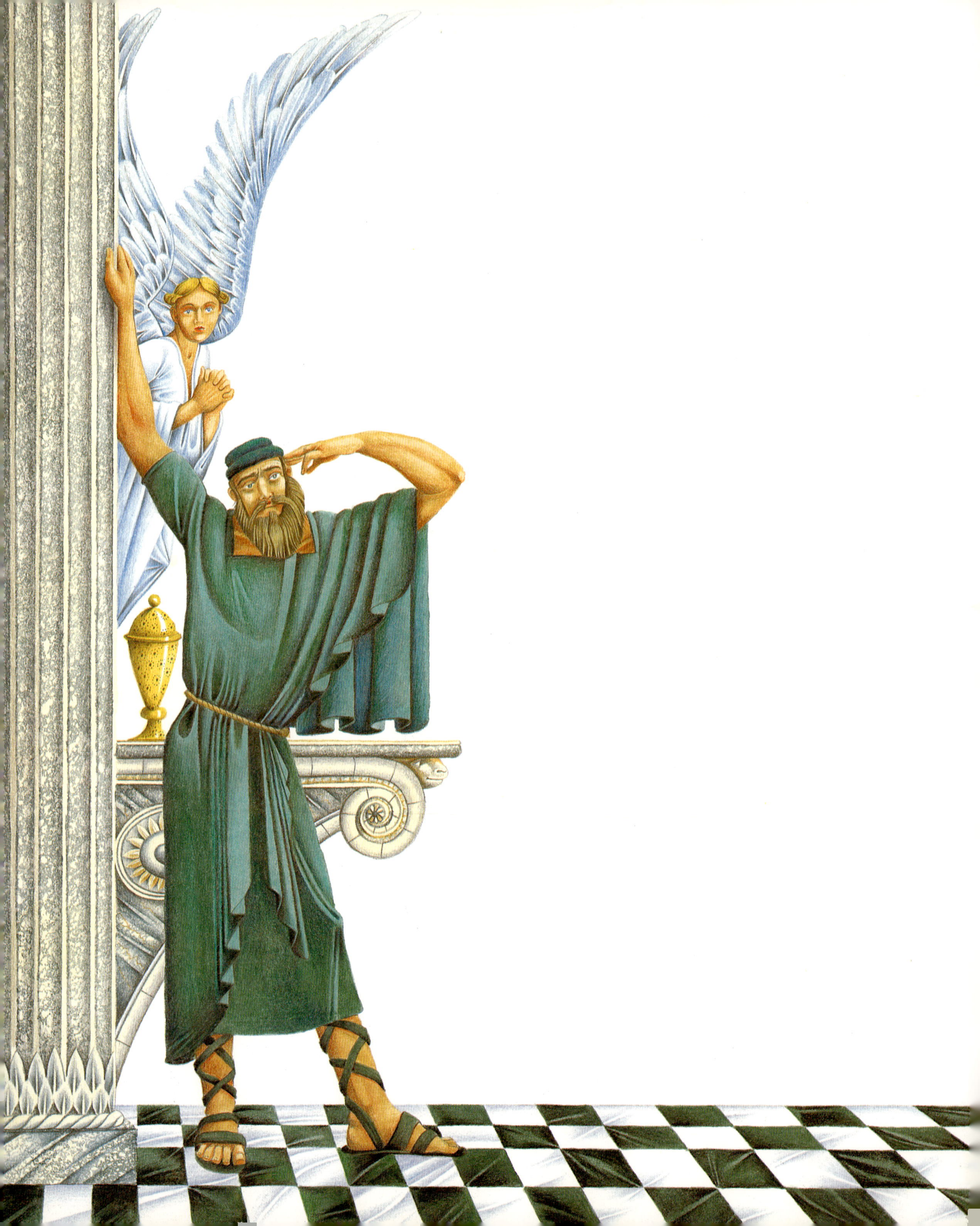

ZACHARIAS, A JEWISH priest, and his wife, Elizabeth, were good, devout people and obeyed all of God's commandments, but they were growing old and had no children.

One day it was Zacharias' turn to burn incense in the holiest sanctuary of the temple. Suddenly, an angel appeared by the altar. Zacharias was gripped with fear, but the angel said:

"Do not be afraid, for your prayer has been heard. Elizabeth will have a son, and you are to name him John. He will be a delight to you, and many people will rejoice, for he will be great in God's eyes. He will be filled with God's Holy Spirit. He will bring many people back to loving the Lord, their God. He will bring parents and children together and bring goodness and wisdom to the disobedient. He will prepare people for the coming of the Lord."

Zacharias asked, "How can I be sure of this? I am an old man, and my wife is well on in years." The angel answered,

"I stand in the presence of God, and I have been sent to tell you this good news. Now you will be unable to speak until all these things have come about, for you did not believe my words."

Meanwhile, the people were wondering why Zacharias had stayed in the temple for so long. When he came out at last, they guessed that he had seen a vision within, for he made signs to them but remained speechless.

His temple duty over, Zacharias returned home and Elizabeth conceived a child. "The Lord has done this for me," she said to herself. "He has taken away the barrenness which made me ashamed."

After about six months, God sent his angel, Gabriel, to a young girl named Mary, who was engaged to a man named Joseph. Joseph was descended from the great King David.

"Hail, you who are most highly favored!" said the angel. "The Lord is with you. You are the happiest of all women."

Mary was troubled and wondered what such words could mean. But the angel said to her, "Fear not, for you have found favor with God. Behold, you will bear a Son, and you will call Him Jesus. The Lord God will give Him the throne of His ancestor, David, and He shall reign over His people forever. His kingdom shall never end. The Spirit of God will come upon you, and the power of God will overshadow you, so that the Holy Child which you will bear will be called the Son of God. And see, your cousin, Elizabeth, whom everyone thought unable to have children, has also conceived a son in her old age, and this is the sixth month for her! For with God, nothing is impossible."

And Mary said, "See me here — I am the handmaiden of the Lord. Let it all happen to me as you have said."

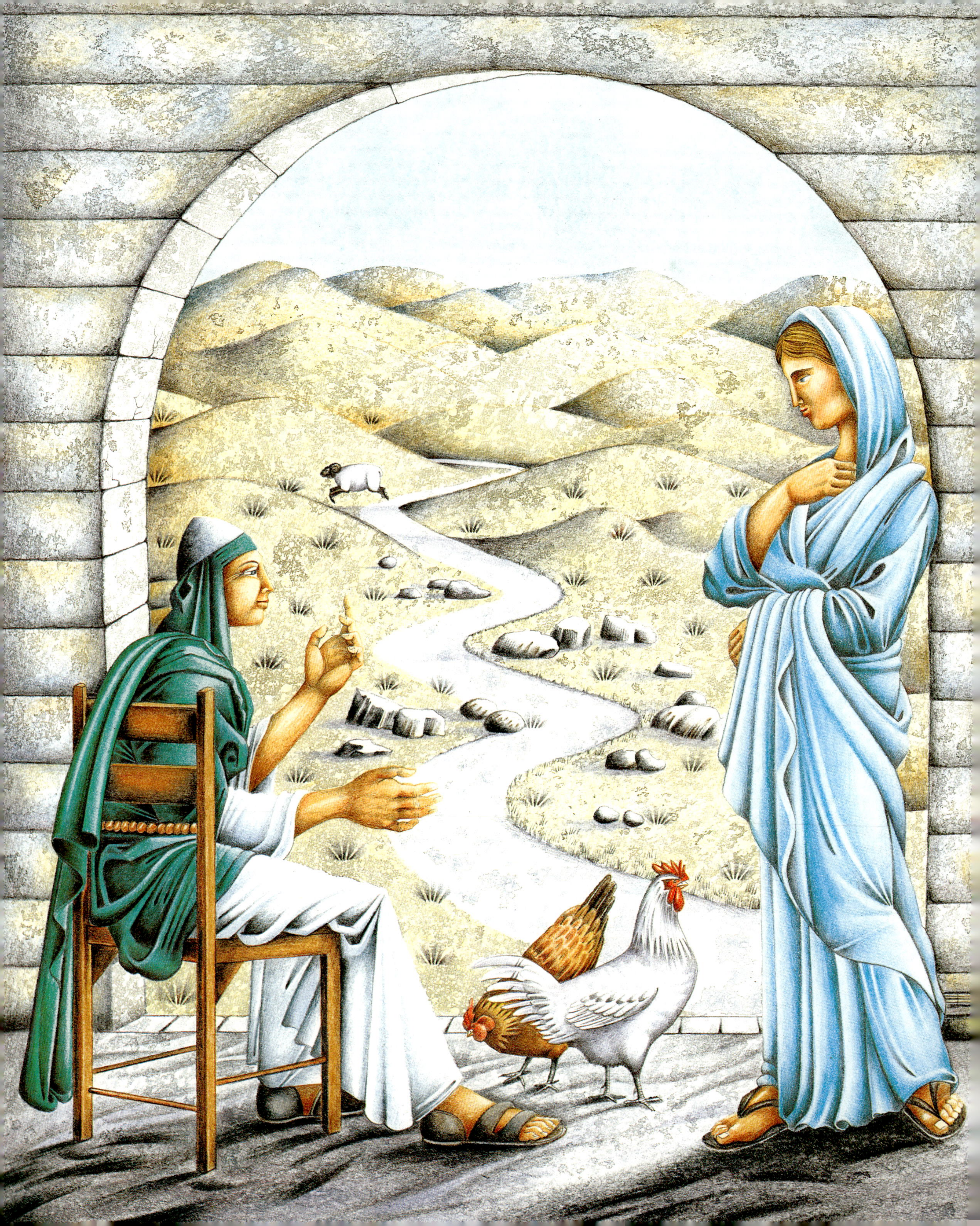

So Mary journeyed into the hill country, to the home of Elizabeth and Zacharias, and as she called her greeting, the baby inside Elizabeth leaped, and she was filled with the Holy Spirit.

"Happy is the child within your womb!" she said. "But who am I, that the mother of my Lord should come to me? How happy she is who believed God!"

And Mary said:

> "My soul magnifies the Lord,
> And my spirit has rejoiced in God, my Saviour.
> For He has regarded the lowly state of His maidservant;
> For behold, henceforth all generations will call me blessed.
> For He who is mighty has done great things for me,
> And holy is His name.
> And His mercy is on those who fear Him.
> From generation to generation.
> He has shown strength with His arm;
> He has scattered the proud in the imagination of their hearts.
> He has put down the mighty from their thrones,
> And exalted the lowly.
> He has filled the hungry with good things,
> And the rich He has sent away empty.
> He has helped His servant Israel,
> In remembrance of His mercy,
> As He spoke to our fathers,
> To Abraham and to his seed forever."

MARY STAYED with Elizabeth until the baby was born. All her family and friends heard how the Lord had been good to her, and they shared her joy. They wanted to call the child after his father, but his mother said, "No! He shall be called John." They said, "But no one in your family is called that!" And they asked his father, who wrote "His name is John." Immediately, his tongue was freed, and he began to speak again.

"And you, child, will be called the prophet of the Highest;
For you will go before the face of the Lord to prepare His ways,
To give knowledge of salvation to His people
By the remission of their sins,
Through the tender mercy of our God,
With which the Dayspring from on high has visited us;
To give light to those who sit in darkness and the shadow
 of death,
To guide our feet into the way of peace."

J ESUS WAS NOT truly the son of Joseph, but according to Jewish law was descended through Joseph from Abraham and David (as the Messiah was promised to be) because Joseph was His adopted father.

Joseph was horrified to find that Mary was going to have a baby. But he was a good, kind man, and he did not want her to be disgraced in the eyes of all the townspeople, so he made up his mind to break the engagement quietly.

But the angel of the Lord appeared to him in a dream, saying, "Do not be afraid to take Mary as your wife, for the Child within her was conceived by the Holy Spirit. She will give birth to a Son, and you will call Him 'Jesus' (which means 'God saves'), because He will save His people from their sins."

All this came to pass, just as God had spoken by the prophet Isaiah, who said, "The virgin will be with child, and will give birth to a Son, and they shall call Him 'Immanuel' (which means 'God with us')."

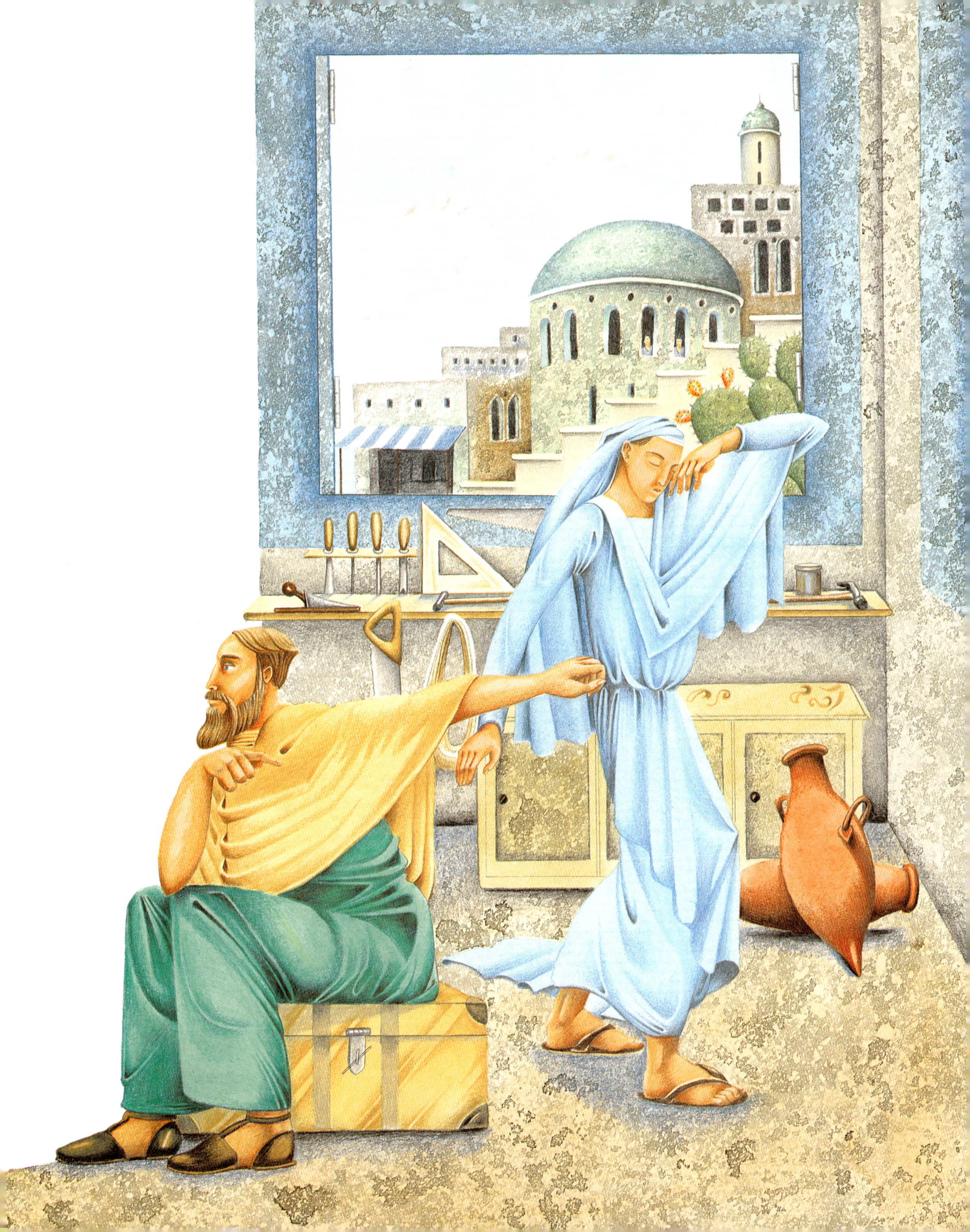

THE GREAT Roman Emperor announced that all of his subjects, even in the little country of Israel, must pay their taxes. Joseph had to go to his family's home town of Bethlehem in Judea, the town of David, to register his name. He took Mary too, and she bore their firstborn Son there. The town was so crowded that there was no room for them in the inn.

There were shepherds in that same country, keeping watch over their flocks by night. Suddenly, the angel of the Lord came to them, and the glory of the Lord shone round about them.

"Fear not," said the angel, "for see, I bring you good news of great joy, which shall be for all people. For this day a Savior has been born — Christ the Lord. You will find the baby wrapped in swaddling clothes, lying in a manger!" And suddenly there was a multitude of heavenly angels praising God:

"Glory to God in the highest,
And on earth peace, good will toward men!"

The shepherds came and found Mary and Joseph and the baby and told all the neighbors about the angel's words. Then they returned, praising God for all they had heard and seen.

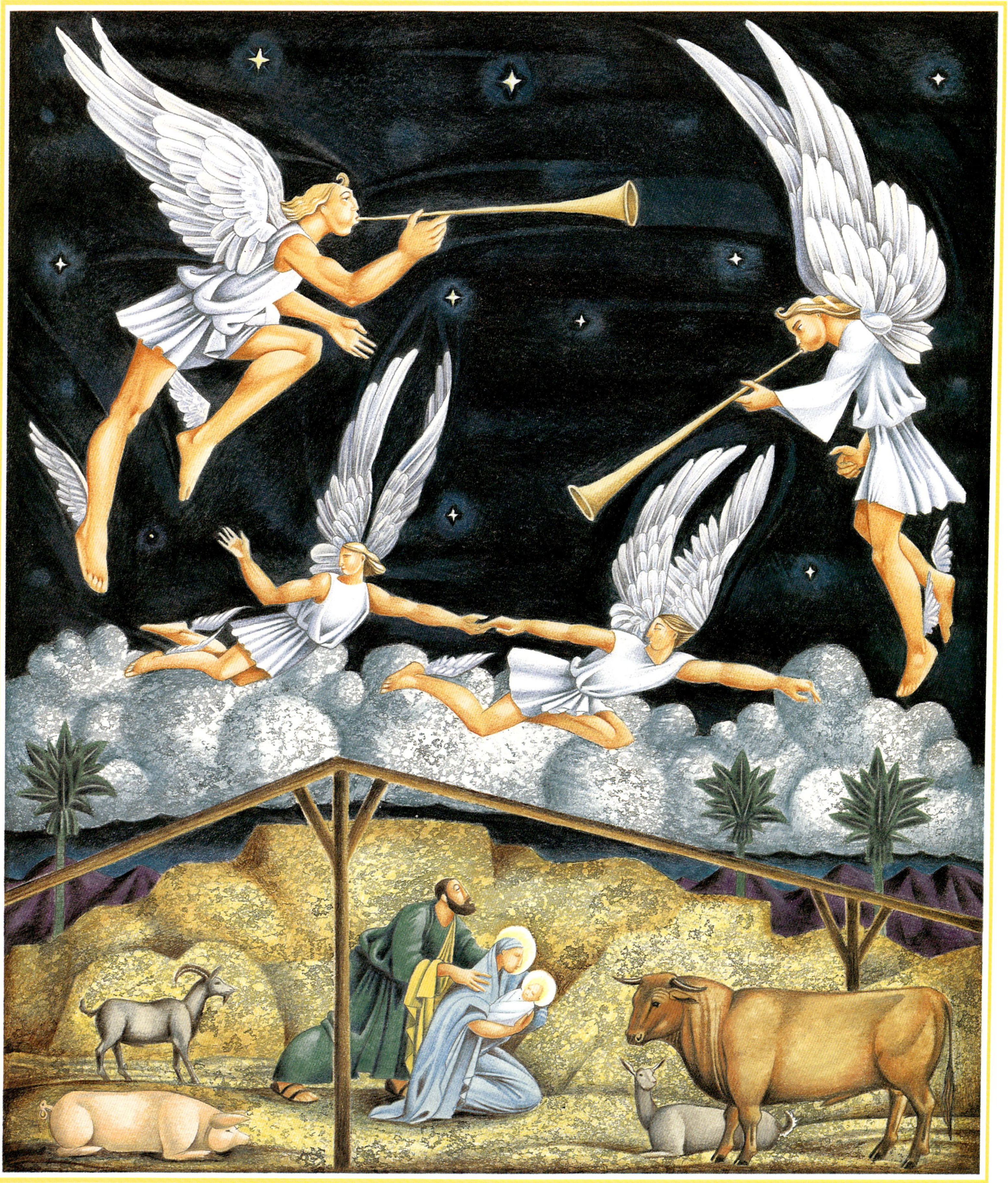

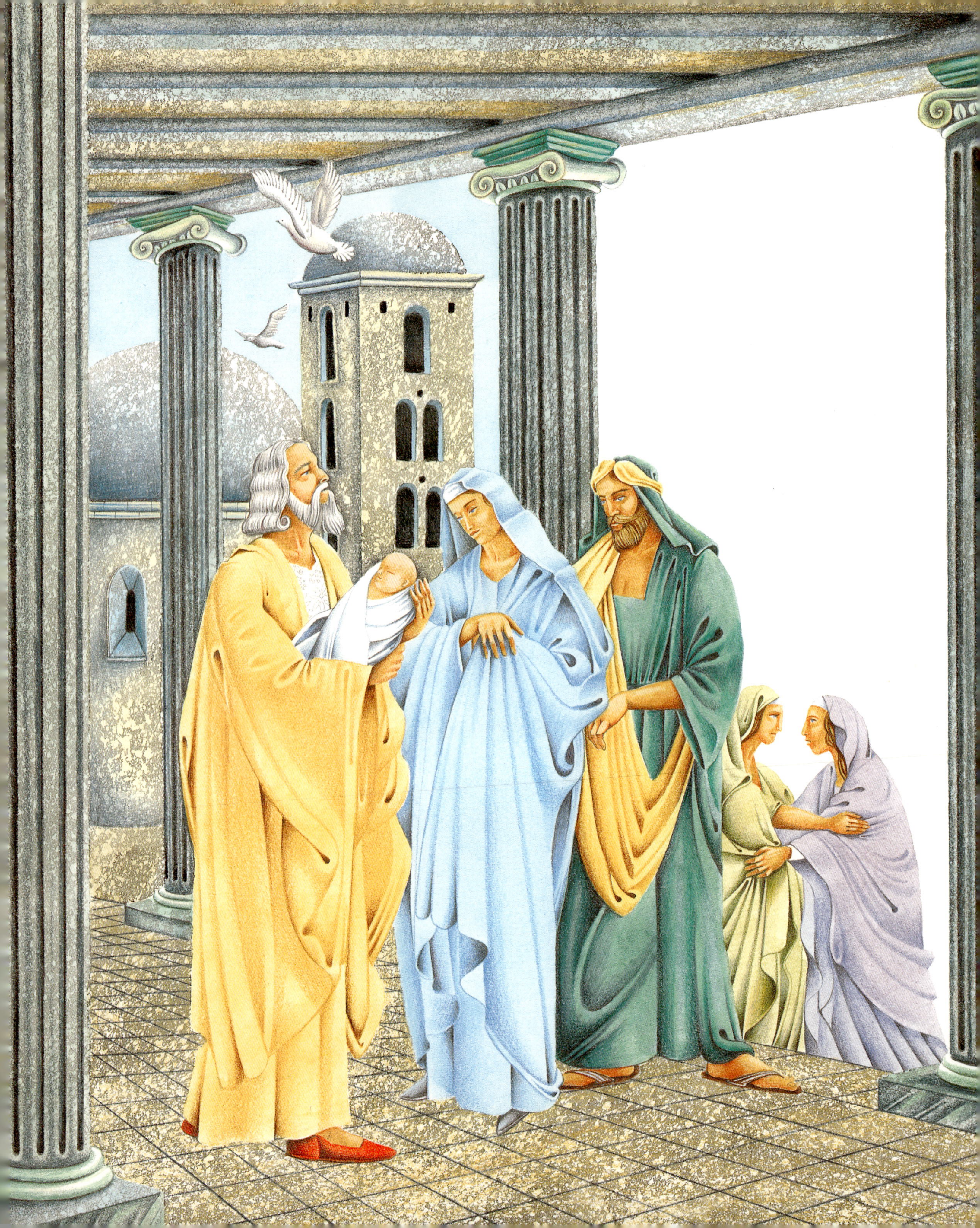

Wheel the child was eight days old he was given the name "Jesus," and Mary and Joseph brought the baby to Jerusalem to present Him to the Lord.

Now there was a man in Jerusalem called Simeon, one of the few who kept hoping and praying that the Messiah would come, and he was full of the Spirit of God. It was revealed to him by the Holy Spirit that he would not die before he had seen the Lord's Christ, the Savior. Led by the Spirit, Simeon went into the temple and took the baby in his arms, blessed God, and said,

> "Lord, now You are letting Your servant depart in peace,
> According to Your word;
> For my eyes have seen Your salvation
> Which You have prepared before the face of all the peoples,
> A light to bring revelation to the Gentiles,
> And the glory of Your people Israel."

Then Simeon blessed them and said to Mary, "See, this Child is destined to cause the fall and rising of many people in Israel, a sign that many will speak against, so that the thoughts of many hearts will be revealed. And a sword shall pierce your own soul also."

And there was a prophetess called Anna, who never left the temple, but served God with fasting and prayer night and day. Now she too came in at that moment and gave thanks to the Lord, speaking of Jesus to all those who were waiting for the Savior.

No ONE KNOWS whether the personages were really kings or wise men, philosophers who studied the stars. But whoever they were, their gifts are symbols of royalty, prayer and death. Strange gifts for a poor baby, but fitting for one who was to become the King of all kings, the one who would rebuild the bridge between God and man, and die for the sake of all people.

They came to Jerusalem asking, "Where is the one who is born to be King of the Jews? We have seen his star in the east, and have come to worship him." When King Herod heard this, he was troubled, gathered all the chief priests and teachers of the law, and demanded where the Savior was to be born. They said, "In Bethlehem, for the prophet Micah wrote,

*'But you, Bethlehem, in the land of Judah,
Are not the least among the rulers of Judah;
For out of you shall come a Ruler
Who will shepherd my people Israel.'"*

Then Herod questioned the wise men about when the star had appeared and sent them to Bethlehem, saying, "Make a thorough search, and when you have found Him, send me news, so that I too can come and worship Him." They left and the star guided them until it came to rest over where the young Child was.

They fell on their knees and worshiped the Child. Opening their bags of treasure, they presented Him with gold, frankincense, and myrrh. Then they returned to their own country by another way, for God had warned them not to go back to Herod.

AFTER THE wise men had gone, the angel of the Lord came to Joseph in a dream, saying,

"Rise up, take the young Child and His mother, and flee to Egypt, and stay there until I tell you, for Herod will search for the young Child to kill Him."

When Joseph woke up, he took the young Child and His mother and left for Egypt that night. (They stayed there until Herod died, and this explains why the prophet Hosea said, "Out of Egypt have I called my son.")

When Herod saw that the wise men had fooled him, he flew

into a furious rage. Remembering the wise men's responses to his questions about when the star had appeared, Herod determined that Jesus was no older than two years of age. The king ordered that children who were under two years old in Bethlehem and in neighboring districts be put to death. Then the words of Jeremiah the prophet came true:

> "A voice was heard in Ramah,
> Lamentation, weeping, and great mourning —
> Rachel weeping for her children,
> Refusing to be comforted, because they were no more."

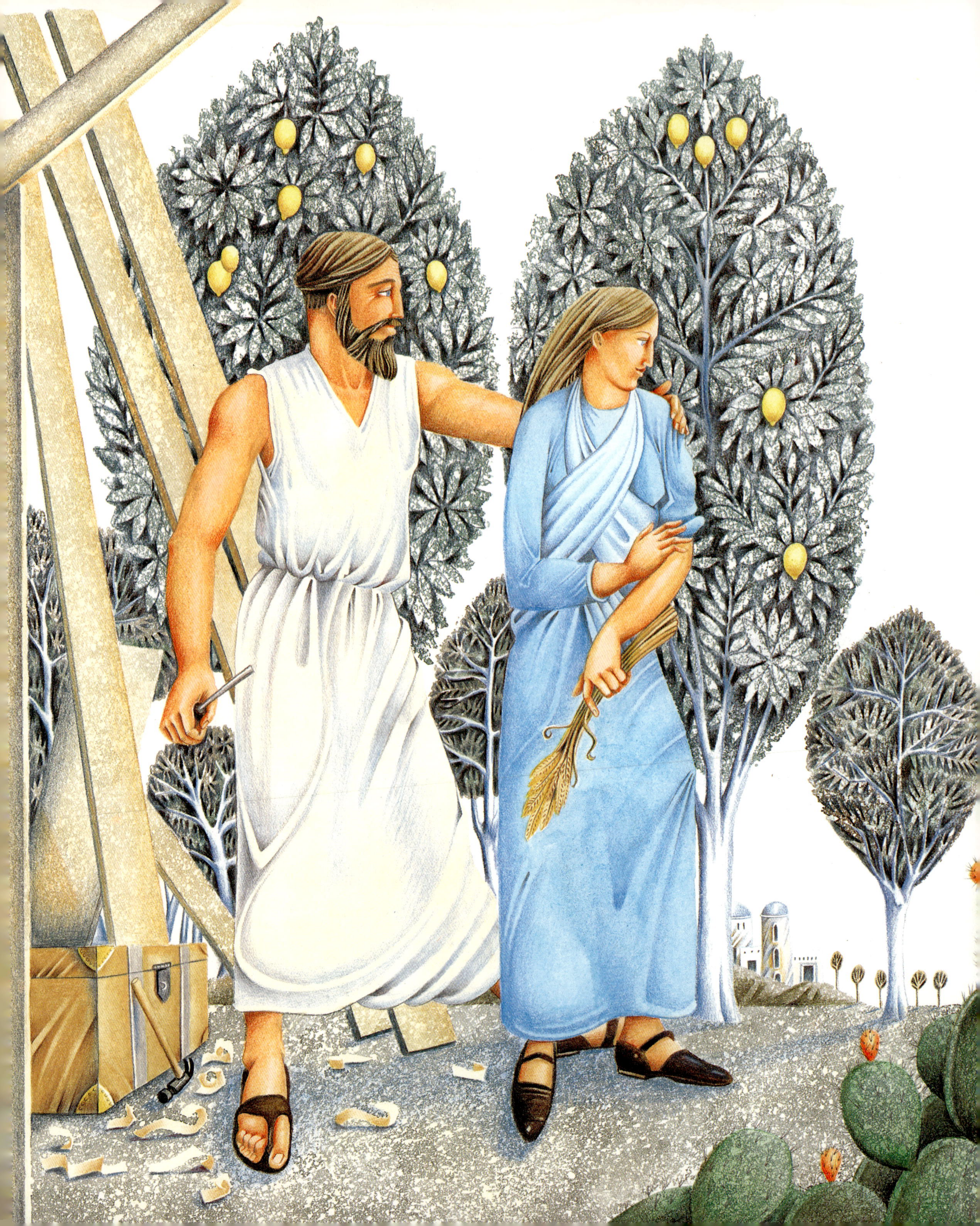

WHEN HEROD died, an angel of the Lord appeared in a dream to Joseph in Egypt, saying,

"Rise up, take the young Child and His mother, and go back to the land of Israel, for the men who wanted to kill the Child are dead."

So Joseph rose, took the young Child and His mother and came back to the land of Israel. But when he heard that Archelaus, the son of Herod, was the king in Judea, Joseph was afraid to go there. Instead, being warned by God in a dream, he went away to Galilee, and settled in a town called Nazareth.

In Nazareth, Jesus grew in wisdom and strength, loved by God and all who knew Him.

Copyright © 1991 Hunt & Thorpe
Text © 1991 by Fiona MacMath
Illustrations © 1991 by Francesca Pelizzoli
Originally published in the UK by Hunt & Thorpe 1991
ISBN 0-8407-9607-2

All rights reserved. Written permission must be secured
from the publisher to use or reproduce any part of this book,
except for brief quotations in critical reviews or articles.

Published in Nashville, Tennessee, by Oliver-Nelson, Inc.,
and distributed in Canada by Lawson Falle, Ltd., Cambridge,
Ontario.

Scripture quotations are from the New King James Version
of the Bible. Copyright © 1979, 1980, 1982, Thomas Nelson, Inc.,
Publishers.

Manufactured in Singapore.

1 2 3 4 5 6 7 – 96 95 94 93 92 91